Other
Times,
Midnight

ABOUT THE LEXI RUDNITSKY FIRST BOOK PRIZE IN POETRY

The Lexi Rudnitsky First Book Prize in Poetry is a collaboration between Persea Books and the Lexi Rudnitsky Poetry Project. It sponsors the annual publication of a collection by a female-identifying poet who has yet to publish a full-length poetry book.

Lexi Rudnitsky (1972–2005) grew up outside of Boston. She studied at Brown University and Columbia University, where she wrote poetry and cultivated a profound relationship with a lineage of women poets that extends from Muriel Rukeyser to Heather McHugh. Her own poems exhibit both a playful love of language and a fierce conscience. Her writing appeared in *The Antioch Review, Columbia: A Journal of Literature and Art, The Nation, The New Yorker, The Paris Review, Pequod*, and *The Western Humanities Review*. In 2004, she won the Milton Kessler Memorial Prize for Poetry from *Harpur Palate*. Lexi died suddenly in 2005, just months after the birth of her first child and the acceptance for publication of her first book of poems, *A Doorless Knocking into Night* (Mid-List Press, 2006). The Lexi Rudnitsky First Book Prize in Poetry was founded to memorialize her and to promote the type of poet and poetry in which she so spiritedly believed.

Previous winners of the Lexi Rudnitsky First Book Prize in Poetry

2023   Raisa Tolchinsky / *Glass Jaw*
2022   Shawn R. Jones / *Date of Birth*
2021   Anni Liu / *Border Vista*
2020   Sarah Matthes / *Town Crier*
2019   Sara Wainscott / *Insecurity System*
2018   Valencia Robin / *Ridiculous Light*
2017   Emily Van Kley / *The Cold and the Rust*
2016   Molly McCully Brown / *The Virginia State Colony for Epileptics and Feebleminded*
2015   Kimberly Grey / *The Opposite of Light*
2014   Susannah Nevison / *Teratology*
2013   Leslie Shinn / *Inside Spiders*
2012   Allison Seay / *To See the Queen*
2011   Laura Cronk / *Having Been an Accomplice*
2010   Cynthia Marie Hoffman / *Sightseer*
2009   Alexandra Teague / *Mortal Geography*
2008   Tara Bray / *Mistaken for Song*
2007   Anne Shaw / *Undertow*
2006   Alena Hairston / *The Logan Topographies*

Other Times, Midnight

Andrea Ballou

A Karen & Michael Braziller Book
PERSEA BOOKS / NEW YORK

Persea Books, Inc.
90 Broad Street
New York, NY 10004

LIBRARY OF CONGRESS CATALOGING-IN-PUBLICATION DATA

Names: Ballou, Andrea, author.
Title: Other times, midnight / Andrea Ballou.
Description: New York : Persea Books, 2025. | "A Karen & Michael Braziller book". | Summary: "Winner of the 2024 Lexi Rudnitsky First Book Prize in Poetry"—Provided by publisher.
Identifiers: LCCN 2024056642 (print) | LCCN 2024056643 (ebook) | ISBN 9780892556083 (paperback; acid-free paper) | ISBN 9780892556090 (ebook)
Subjects: LCGFT: Poetry.
Classification: LCC PS3602.A625 O84 2025 (print) | LCC PS3602.A625 (ebook) | DDC 811/.6—dc23/eng/20241125
LC record available at https://lccn.loc.gov/2024056642
LC ebook record available at https://lccn.loc.gov/2024056643

Book design and composition by Rita Skingle
Typeset in Arno Pro
Manufactured in the United States of America. Printed on acid-free paper.

for Hannah, Alex, and Jack

CONTENTS

I.

II.

III.

IV.

The odd sound. What a mercy to have that to turn to.
   —SAMUEL BECKETT

I.

—

Family Business

Everyone in my house has a ripped face.
My job is to re-upholster them.
I use matches, needles, coat hangers—

whatever gets the job done.

I don't enjoy this work.
It is difficult.

Everyone has a hat and a foil-lined
bed full of rocks.

Also I have a doll.
I keep her in a walled
garden. She wears a metal bowl
on her head. Long ago she stopped

thinking and sits alone
under a silvery tree.

The ship docks over there, in a separate corner.

We all go on the ship.
We rip our faces.
We wash up on the beach.

Every day we play this game.
It's called house or
sometimes
we don't name it.

It Helps if You Name It

And so he died, and so Diana's anger was satisfied at last.
    —OVID

How she, in that moment, unloads her other cargo, her rage

onto what's-his-name

is only half the story. Other half pulled

apart from the world, bereaved.

His dream of saving (seeing) her becomes her own dream.

She hunts down the world's refinery. The heart of it.

*

Worst day of my life, alone in a big house near the sea.

I have to understand what I want.

Destroy is hard to say.

Bereavement? Rage? Town-like venom, and then

I find myself tracking some sea creature, arched

spine against the blue sky.

*

Past the bridge, near it, near his house
could have

(too late?)

seen him. Wants to understand

what she wants, what

she wanted. Build

or sail?

(deflowered)

What flower?

Her brain.

*

What is called thinking? Blue rag. Bow and arrow.

*

Her vault needs work, it's only

half as tall now, paved—

no fault but her own—dragged a table saw
through her own window—

(o the brevity of it) destruction
of the body—her rage,

(no, her wrath)

then next day

sky—and its walkways.

*

All the work of living in the arch itself,

inside of it,

I call thinking—work of the mind, that swaggery

abdomen, how it maneuvers.

*

I name myself. What's my name?

Stump-Mover.
Fence-Lifter.
Dread-of-Thousands.

*

From the barge you will see my eight bridges.

Is this a true story? (I've spilled parts of it)

6

The story is not hard. The trickiest part is thinking

back to the road. My car on it.

*

You want to let everyone know how you will save
what's-his-name, that strange
piece of yourself you find missing.

You are tracked
and tracker. Inside the arch itself, even with art, sky

is hard to say. Look here, don't trade your brain

for anything except a ruin. Because destroy
is always harder to say.

To understand what you want is the trickiest kind of thinking.

(rivets a wax wing onto the back of her bird)

What's-his-name has a heart of red feathers (she wants it).

(she wants it like she wants her car, for the way it moves)

You want to let everyone know about the work you are doing,
the color of it.

(takes a sharp right out to sea, her cargo—nails and lumber of
the so-called modern era—needs a complete overhaul including
window replacements)

*

What's-his-name is someone I want.

I want his feathered heart.

I want my bridges.

I want a job.

No one, anymore, says strange.

No one says tank farm, or bereavement, or refinery.

(going through the list again of possible jobs)

It must involve thinking. Vault. Blue rag. Maybe exile.
(four pairs of eyes, four men nearby, his friends,

watch the dogs devour what's-his-name)

I want a letter opener. Envelopes.

I no longer have a car. What I need now is a sickle.

*

What's-his-name says this is the worst day of his life. O his dogs.

No one will deny that.

His four friends walk out of the forest back to their cars.

She hungers for the yellow fields. Thinks of him

in that big house near the sea, alone now. Destroyed.

O the venom, the strange tracking,

the rage she felt—over what? Her vault—

the road goes right through her archway,

(she fans herself out)

all kinds of creatures breaching her walls.

*

I want a job—the narrowest of bridges.

(takes a sharp right)

I have to decide, do I want a bridge
or a car?

Do I want in the world—as in,
live-in-it? Or just

a brief visit.

Do I want to live with what's-his-name in that big house near the sea?

In the arch—or on the road now? Or, all of it.

Destroy is half the work I call thinking, where I find myself

tracking the strange, wooden job
of being human. Is there any such thing as a heart-brain,

color of the road, sky (most powerful of all cargo).

Listen,
love calls us near-to-it, or

you-are-so-close.

I've said enough. How do I love more.

Love better and still
keep all my equipment, see

all eight of my bridges intact.

Shed Boat Shed

Last week I heaved myself into the shed,
tucked in with roofing nails, hammers, and tins of ham
and—guess what! you were there too, surrounded
by four angels beating their leather wings. They deliberated
you, massaged your legs; the wind had freshened
the left half of your face and the angels said to themselves
He turns out to be short, but not incapable of flourishing;
they scraped you open, saw your right hand
was withered—that's what they called it.
                              Outside, a squeaky wind
pump. Tucked inside a hawthorn bush behind it
a small bird ate without speaking. No air, no one about.
You hardly moved. Bits of waiting; the smell of something small
and dead. I'd come close to drowning—thrashed
the brown water with my own small and ineffective wings;
I'd barely pulled my full-length self out of the river.
                      The day was exceptionally quiet. Ordinary.
Today, though, is another story. Alongside the four angels,
four hundred souls fill the shed up to its roof. I pull out
my bread. Inside my timbers I eat without speaking and watch
as you begin to heave.

What the Wooden Duck Says
When I Can't Sleep at Night

1.

What kind of word are you looking for?

An ice-age word, or pre-Columbian,
something with feathers on it.

How about flannel?

Or sandpaper?

How about instead we turn on the Weather Channel.

(I've decided not to listen to the decoy—
hand-carved or not.)

*I see a declarative sentence in your future—
something bold, with a little malice in it.*

(I look straight ahead at the TV.)

War!

How about remorse?
The aftermath of anything
is more compelling.

Yes, a different bird entirely.

(The blasted duck is merciless,
harbors toward me a sort of ill will
disguised as charity.)

2.

Any successful thoughts yet?

No, I'm dried up.

You need another word already?

I thought you were going to sleep.

Here's a sentence for you—
In my generation
you went wherever he had a job—

the old "whither thou goest—"

You know I hate traveling.

I blinked on the train once.
Ended up alone and barefoot
outside the village of Calasanz,
irrigating potato fields for strangers.

Dig deeper! they shouted
waving their hoes in the air.

Is that what you're looking for—
a whole story?

No, just a few good tubers.

3.

You awake? Got
another one—

Beckoning Sea.

Not meant for me—
I'm landlocked.

(The duck talks
in his sleep,
dreams of the sea.)

So after the crackdown
was that you singing

behind the chicken coop?

4.

Remorse docked her boat
long ago on my shore.
The sea

Is that you singing?

beckoned and beckoned
until I could not
resist

the vast, salted fields

Is that you singing?

the handcarts listing with sod.

We kneel

Behind the chicken coop
is that you singing?

beside your open grave,
a wound that will not close.

At supper
we eat eggs

Is that you singing?

from a single white hen.

Foxes slip into the house
at night—
another song departs, departs.

Is that you?

Oh how I miss you

my tender violet
my downy chick

Remorse Is a Place Made of Little Boxes of Sound

On the baby's fifth day
critical aortic stenosis
bicuspid valve surgeon says,

open heart
blindness, brain damage

50-50 chance

Of what, I say

                          *

(from inside the box) I say

            maybe it would be better
            to begin again

no, wait

            better to die first
            and begin again

wait, say

            better
            for this baby to die—
            and you and I begin again

*

I cannot close

      this sorry box, can never

unsay it

*

(long time   no sound

      only
      breathing)

start
running running running

*

out the narrow gate

back to the boat I came on
iron body

iron box
my habitat
my death-door

*

See my bare foot
step into a boat—

as if there were no landscape
Keep going, cries the family

*

I calculate my losses—

gone the stone house
gone the sheltering wood
small family also gone

No one calls from the forest

*

The door bangs open, shut
(low tide again)

I wrap twig fingers
over my eyes, practice dying

*

How closely this child
resembles time

She has a voice
with three layers of hair

has a voice
like a long, thin wire

*

In a boat on a yellow sea
rain falls from a cloudless sky

My finger traces
the six-inch scar down her chest

scar says *be quiet,*
be quiet now

*

Stones drop
one by one
into the water

*

All the apples
I've ever eaten

I keep in a green
metal box

next to my bed,
like dolls—each one

has a name
Where are you, they say

We have nothing to eat

Don't worry, I say
I would never

let you starve

Sometimes, winter

other times, midnight

its belly is not
so bitter
is handcrafted

my own belly
lights and crackles

death, if I can persuade myself,
is a great thought

(so long, she says
lowering her eyes

past the hut
past the tall gray rock
the forest)

the reason was not soon
the reason was not the forest
the reason was not the oarsman

(it is not so hard to imagine)

the reason is I saw myself
crackle and weep
by the edge of the stream

that bitter day
that tall gray rock

(rejoice, she says
lowering her eyes)

death, lowering now its own belly
has no great thoughts

other times, light

other times, rejoice

other times, water

(so long, she says

so long, forest

so long, bitter day

so long, oarsman)

in the mouth of midnight
my story

is brittle, delicate

beautiful?

not so

other times, maybe

soon it will be midnight

soon it will be beautiful

II.

Love Inside the Snow Globe

Every day we drive
early to the airport
with a white chicken
in the back seat

It takes all day
to get there
I drop you off
and you fly somewhere
icy

On the way home
my brother drives
while I hold
the chicken
in the back seat

We wait
at the intersection
close to home

Intersect
says my brother
means to cut
asunder
cut off
one field from another

I hold the chicken
tight
I pluck her feathers
and paste them
all over myself

The chicken and I
are white carpet
and snow
we are two crystals

Retrato de viuda con caballero andante

One spring my husband departs,

        right out the kitchen window.

Back soon, he says,

      fastening his armor.

Okay, I say.   Now off

      he goes. I wait

            and wait. Winter arrives. Snow falls

for months. No, years. By this time

      I am asleep

            on a glacier.

Okay, finally

      I wake up.   *Yoohoo—*

nothing happens—not a sound.

So.

      I tidy up the place, rebuild the shed, the chicken coop,

take up needlepoint, tire of it, think

                                        Wait! Why

        waste my time
                        with housework when in winter

            it's birds everywhere!

Cardinals, bullfinches, blackbirds out my kitchen window—

        there they go   defending territory
attracting mates.

I memorize medieval ballads—knights riding up on horseback,

                        home from the war. The husband always

unfamiliar, unrecognizable. Or

                unrecognized.   Big difference.

Catalina, under a laurel,

        next to a stream, daydreams, watches the water

            the knight rides slowly by on his horse, her reverie

broken. Flags him down—

        Have you seen my husband?

No—what does he look like?

Oh he's tall and blond, handsome like you

etcetera

Ah yes, he was killed by a colonel.
Asked me to marry you in his place.

Oh no, I would never marry you,
not in seven years, never! I'd sooner send
my daughter to the convent and my sons to the king.

In some versions of the ballad

    she resists the knight's advance.   But! Here comes

what's always troubled me—the husband reveals himself

    in the last stanza, calls her
by name

Calla, calla, Catalina
Calla, calla de una vez,
Que estás hablando con tu marido
Y no lo sabes reconocer,
Que estás hablando con tu marido
Y no lo sabes reconocer.

So. It was a test. Look

how he sneaks his way
                  back in through the window. She knew all along
           it was him.

Anyway, spring comes. I ready the flowerbeds. I plant

          peonies, snapdragons, creeping

thyme. The neighbors see me alone in the garden,
                  take pity, bring

pot roast, casseroles, cherry cobbler. At the bar

they meet for cocktails, hash over my so-called widowhood—

          they relish this topic. Husbands offer

                  to fix my roof, my plumbing. I don't tell them

I hear you call from far away,

after nightfall, like some nighthawk flying over the forest canopy.

On the day you arrive and I'm seated under a tree,

                  say, the apple, or the white oak (my favorite)

and you ride up on your horse, and you take off your armor

I will ask you

     for news of my husband. How

romantic
        would that be.

.

A Brief History of War,
from Rome to the Present Day

I'll give you a goose
if you carry me all the way back to camp
in your chariot, she says.

He goes off to think about it,
returns with a wooden sword
in his scabbard.

You twisted little devil, he says.

A flock of wildfowl lands on the plain.

We can't part like this, she says.
Her long brown skirts flap
like birds' wings.

He waves his sword—
That's better! he says,
now let's
have a fight with rules.

She fletches her arrows.
Whose rules, she says.

The flock lifts and scatters
into the western sky.

The end.

Sunset.

Portrait of Soldier with Mind Ajar

for Thomas Henry Keogh (b. Thurles, Ireland 1859,
d. Medfield State Hospital, Medfield, Massachusetts, 1930)

Thomas marvels, his mind races

        backwards across the horizontal

slip of window. He is old
    and soon to be posthumous.

    We've collapsed, he says, unhinged

from empire.

Dishes clatter in the kitchen—Thomas Henry's mind goes directly

    outside, walks through tilled fields

to the woods and tells itself
    a story about the old days—

 I was with my comrades. We drank
    milk from wooden buckets—

he tries hard to remember
        the definition of victory
and cannot—

    we traveled single file through the forests, like deer—

Furtive. *No,*
      restless.

In his mind he staples stars

onto loaves of bread, loads them onto wheelbarrows
        bound for the newly divided city.

    oh we wept! and wept
But who will eat your bread, Thomas? You are desolate now—a
    sliver,
                a gesture
        amen
he says through his eyes, through his two empty windows in flames.

He begins to write everything down on the insides
                        of matchbooks he will burn later—

We disguised ourselves as allies—lived

        on the run—ate nothing

                but the fruit at our fingertips.

No, Thomas   you are wind

you are disguised now as a thin
                        sliver of wind.

Oh Thomas Henry a thought tightens
        your brain—what's the right way

to describe what's happened

the right way to say committed or
       war crimes

       thereafter,   some thoughts

         (little wings)

therefore leather tendrils, then
               theft.

What use is your brain now, your flower

says the angel whose face has recently been uncovered

the angel who ushered in your defeat
your dereliction
your dismay

         the angel who says
Thomas you can't sleep

         the angel who builds
the tiny wooden shacks

         the angel who looks like a hermit

         the angel who lights
a fire and drinks tea

         the angel who eats porridge

         the angel who is incomplete

and treacherous

         the angel who caught you
laughing

         the angel who folds his wings
upon your forehead

         the angel who will not let you rest

         the angel who says *Thomas*
who did you kill today

         the angel who pulls
a lead curtain across your brain

         the angel who says
I love you Thomas you're unhinged

you are one-of-a-kind

you are a pleated book Thomas
     a lame beggar
     a leather worker
     a dead enemy

you are a window frame
         ablaze

         the angel who sees you
entering
    and leaving

the angel who beats

his muscular wings

his wings of needles
his terrifying wings
his wings like two wooden doors

two iron lids

touching
touching

then

twilight—

says

vacant—unrelated

to who you were
            before the war,

before the wanderlust

                        set in.

Soldier's Wife in the Aftermath

After the great war I stepped inside
to make sourdough bread.

That's when you vanished, mi amor.

Last I saw, you were inside the cathedral
gnawing on a wooden pew.

I still dream about you.

Why, last night the two of us
were transporting a gigantic, precious sow,
tawny and maned like a lion,
in the back of a blue truck.

Hallelujah! I slap my thigh
just thinking about it.

III.

How We Manage Since Father Died

We have a finch.
Her name is Lucy.
She is a mature deity.

We dress her
in brown leather shoes
and handmade woolens.
We cling to her.

The village has fled insomnia—
some of us hunt,
some weave dresses of yak hair,
others persist in finding a detour.

I've pitched my tent
on the bank of the river,
here, where it bends
to the left then folds

gently in a different direction.
It is a protective river—
a catastrophic river.

I cover myself in pitch.
I weave grass through my teeth.

In twelve more hours father
will be nearly soil—

I have almost spent myself.

Famine Road

1.

I will tell you the whole story,

it goes like this—

Once upon a time it was not a fine day.

I see a dark thread running through the cloth of your family.

Yes I know this thread it is crimson.

It's called malaise.

All the women in my family sew.

First thing I hemmed was an apron.

Hazel and my mother still crochet blankets.

No one knits socks anymore.

My grandmother made lace with knots.

That's called tatting.

She had useful fingers.

I want to be useful.

You are a box of tools disguised as a girl.

2.

First there was thread then there was swimming.

There were fish and a crystal clear lake.

The family was flush.

On the wide front of one morning, I wake up.

The forest is bristling.

Will we have enough food today?

Father is not talking.

One of his legs is bent—I see him

through the courtyard gate.

Oh those were the old days, big as dinner plates.

3.

We were traveling east

loaded with tubers.

The ground was saying things again

and we were suffering.

You said—you shall not defile the land

in which you live

in which I also dwell.

Then you said—

Be rain.

Be unshod.

Be unwed.

Remember how you sent us packing,

how we fled.

4.

Run! the children cry. So we run.

Quick, children, find your socks!

We run through the middle of the city,

look for the gate leading out.

5.

I am packed.

Inside myself I hold

like an hour

all the rest.

In the field,

in the vicinity

of things,

the family walks

outside

and I do not.

I am cold.

Inside myself my feet

walk outside.

6.

One night our blessings

crack.

I am cold,

smell of buttermilk and almonds.

That means you are bereft.

Two extra legs

inside myself or

overall—

7.

Say something about the tent.

In the vicinity of supper,

in the field

of things—

always the tent.

Always the tent moving.

Every night I

smell traveling,

pack food.

Inside myself

I take time

for supper—

like an hour.

Life is mild

and arrives.

8.

Let's go ahead and name that place.

Let's name it giant.

No, name it gigantic.

How's my story holding up?

You must order and reorder the woods.

How will I ever name that place
(kinship)

again—

Jack Wonders Why We Call Friday Good

In the beginning was the dove.
The dove was lonely and set out from home.
Watch the lost dove fly out through the open
door of heaven, descend through the dark

bone of space and hover over the water.
See the tendons, the ligaments—all that binds
a body to itself. What binds one body
to another, we call desire. On that day

three sets of fingers reached for each other
over the water and toward the sky—
and behold, speech came into being;

speech, son, is how you bind
what you love to what you don't yet
know to love.

Landscape, Two Windows

Who was I, then

Wife, but

Almost

A landscape, we were

Two windows
Walking together.

For each other, we had names
O Brother of the Sun
O Sister of the Sun
O Beloved
Wasp, Hummingbird, Swamp

Two children in the mouth of an alley

Not portrait, but

Changelings wrapped in tiny wool blankets,

Emaciated. Love covers
A multitude of sins, is its own pavement. I was

All yours, almost

Never.

They Said It Would Hurt, and It Does

I am in a motel.

There's so much to eat here—

dock
nettles
seaweed

Famine food.

You forgot ashes.

*

Ok. A soul cries out to me. I strain to hear it.

Says it wants to live. Leave. I can't tell which.

I say no.

It says bridge, gate. Says flood will do.

I still say no.

It says my heart's become so jagged it cuts flesh.

*

I need a new strategy.
In the motel coffee shop I am rereading *The Art of War*.

I write the word *petrified*, as in my heart. Stone fortress.

*

What pierces best? According to Sun-Tzu, whatever turned
the heart to stone in the first place.

Or maybe I made that up.

O would that stone could liquefy, my heart turn watery, become
the very sea I sail on.

*

Self-portrait. Brackish. Back-looking pillar of salt. Hearth-lover. Exile.

*

The eastern hemlock is dying. This winter a neighbor

wants to cut our small stand.

I say no. I'll watch them die a slow death, anticipate

the forest without them.

*

Nightfall. In *The Art of War*, I read about nine kinds of ground.

On enclosed ground, devise strategies. I fan myself out—wide
bridge to the sea. Not yet sea itself.

On death ground, fight. Here, I am at a loss.

*

Hemlock comes to life in late winter, stabilizes the land. Three years ago father died. Our own herd still wanders, diminished. What will happen

when mother also? I write for the thing that is dying.

*

A crow explodes into the air from the edge of the forest. I am fighting an impulse to not speak.

*

Okay. I am contemplating a vast wall of ovens. My dog

is with me.

A woman wearing a chef's hat and crisp white coat stares me down,

arms crossed, next to the ovens. She nods.

So I cram the dog into a red cooking pot.

He wants to live. What a struggle.

I wake up before I finish. Understand,

it doesn't matter. I'm not writing about the dog.

*

Okay. This is how you leave me. You wander into the air.
I call this a predicament. Or, in a quieter place,

I call it trauma.

*

Do you know what leaving sounds like?

Exactly. I record its aftermath. Hemlocks creaking

in a silent winter wood. Ice crystals forming, or

wood, petrifying.

*

So. Now I am thirsty.

(That means dying, in my language)

Look at me. I've lost my way.

No. You've lost your nerve.

I'll go now.

Go ahead, walk out. That means die, in your language.

*

Not Lot's wife, turned back to see her city in flames. Then, pillar of salt. What did she call herself, if not Lot's wife? I call myself molten.

*

The waitress is asking if I want more coffee.

On the other side of the glass

it is raining. You are leaving.

How do I say

I will miss you, in your language?

Or say, we are a people who pass

from one field to the next,

inarticulate,

desirous? Or

I am with you, and not

with you?

I am trying to say, in any language,

I arrive.

Have arrived just in time to see you pass

into the next field, without me.

IV.

Passover with the Wooden Duck

1.

That evening when I got home
I wrote on my entrance
Look for the scrubland
with a thorn and kohl. When the tattoo

became infected, I wrote a fifty-word story.

I got a call.

Come to the city. We have black tea, six rolls,
and five liters of water.

By morning the ground
felt like a coffin, a ring of legs
collapsing beneath us—

some of us wanted to think of our God.

I sought out a relative
at a military-sponsored destination.

It was a tough day.

2.

Next day, beautiful. Something new.

On Harvest Avenue, I spent the night
in the back of a transport truck
watching the soccer games.

I was frighteningly thin.

The country was frighteningly thin,
like a small grocery store.

After a few months mother comes
to inspect the camp,

says *What you're doing is evil—
behaving thuggishly.*

The country is a giant suitcase
collapsing,
its legs collapsing beneath it.

I put my belongings down
on the train, beside me.
Fans were scattered across the seats,
it was a hot day.

I was not allowed to leave early.

3.

We were just crawling along
fighting for independence.

Think about it, says mother.

We think about it.

I think about it, about what she says.

I think about everything
she says.

4.

Here comes the wooden duck
clapping his beak, his wooden wings.

He's like a slingshot, somehow—
I doubt he will be civil.

Into my cell the light is coming
from a small, high window.

I want to play with the duck,
invent a game. Today he is

serious, turns up his bill
at a spread of solitaire.

I offer him lentil soup
for breakfast—

black tea, six rolls,
five liters of water.

What he wants is a blanket.

5.

Today not good. I'm in trouble
for stealing water.

They beat me with a stick
then put my belongings next to me.

I change clothes.

I tussle with myself.

I cry a little bit—

I am desperate to get home.

6.

My family greets me
with surprise. They stow my bedding
and clothes.

Your pride is oppressed, they say.

The rest of the family sneaks out
to play checkers. I stay inside,
speak with my mother.

Mother, I say, show me the door
to human suffering. Tell me
how people suffer.
Volunteer yourself, she says. *Take a more
aggressive approach.*

I want to be a professional general,
try a wide range
of occupations—mining, farming,
metalworker, leather tanning.

*There's a shortage of all kinds
of trained people.*

Who are people, I ask my mother.

*There's no such thing as people.
There are only neighbors—
try to be flexible about this.*

This upsets the duck.

You may fail the exam, he says.

7.

I think about escaping
the decoy.

I try farming.

You are not farming, you are breaking
stone, says the duck—

picando piedra, nothing more.

I want to look for a secluded café,
an older brother.

I'm just the messenger, says the duck.

8.

I have resettled myself.

I clear the streets,
digging and plowing
for no pay.
I'm in a two hundred-pound mood.

I spend my nights locked up
at the local police station.
On nights off, I work as a guard.
I'm aware this is a double-standard.

At the mall, I score a lot of points.
I am safe—a little food
and water—I am safe.

9.

The duck wants to hatch a plan.

All around me

Keep quiet—give me time to think—

I hear a second chance.

The duck is bearded now,
restless,

looking to cross the Red Sea
immediately.

Hey! don't leave without me—

I'll not write anymore about childhood—yours, mine or
anyone else's.

Son in This Story the Oaks Are Tremendous

I've read of forests that follow rivers
of legendary strength and beauty,

become lost in mist,
cloud forests.

So the first question
is what lost means.

Your orders came today.
You ship out

in the fall. Lost is also
the second question.

I will tell the family
you are cold and afraid.

I will tell myself you have just
reached out and touched your own

story, as if it were
your own manhood.

Wing Man

My brother drives the yellow Ford Fiesta. I am a passenger beside him in the front seat. I want to report to him on my studies, what I've learned abroad in a foreign language. *I've read about life before the apple* I say *and we all know what happened after—it's the apple itself I'd like to know more about.*

We arrive at the waterfront of a small coastal city. He wants to show me his friend's warehouse. I am a grown woman with my own family. My two dogs Louis and Charlie are running in and out of the back seat transported by the brisk air, the fishing boats, the boundless sea and its salty promise. Its durability.

I want to tell my brother about the oracle the wall of words I saw last night in my dream. *Out of the big hand came the small hand and out of the small hand came the big hand.* Instead he opens the back door of my car which he's filled with dead pelicans to teach me a lesson about failure. *Look here!* he says with a flourish, brandishing one of the stiffened birds upside down by a gray leg.

That night Jesus dive bombs my aircraft carrier. We float next to each other, upright. He wears gray khakis, a blue Hanes t-shirt, shops at Walmart like the rest of us. He is handsome and I love him. I hover next to him way above the deck. He says he will demonstrate for me his belly-down landing technique. *It looks preposterous but just watch,* winks, does a belly-smacker onto the landing deck. Everyone thinks he's dead. Including me. He rises up next to me, dives again and lands like a plane. *Now,* he says, so close his arm touches mine, *try flying with your own body.*

Origin of Speech

Whippoorwill pierces the dusk.

A woman undrowns herself.

In the field, a man clothed in leaves comes to life.

Evening, unshod,
leads the field, dragging a letter

hand-written in red.

(Listen, on the hooves of a dream,

      malaise of the red oak

she hears it climb in through the window)

In the village, the shops are broken.
She makes a wide porch tied like a rope

around her waist,

ties the broken shops around her blue and violet waist.

She makes a small wind tower, unfurls the bright unrest.

Unfurls her sound table.

Evening, unshaken and brazen,
rises, unwed,

into the field.

Voice tied like a rope to the dusk.

More Tender, Even, Than Light

We are in a motel. I have a kind of vision, fallen from the sky.

My husband is a rock, sleeping. I leave him and go to sea. I am
starved for air. I sail east. In the six cities of refuge, I staple myself
to trees. I write him many letters. I want to lift up. I call this
painting.

I sail home. My ship is loaded with canvases.

We are two portraits crossing the desert. I ask what he thinks of
the new landscape. *Beautiful,* he says. *What do you call it?*

Water, love. I call it water.

The Blue Hills

A soul on the brink
of leaving the family
headed for the woods
at the end of West Street.

I caught it by the flaps
halfway out the gate,
lured it back indoors.

I fed it potatoes and cabbage,
fish on Fridays.

When the days turned
cool and frost rimed
the windows, I made

the soul a pallet
on the kitchen floor,
near the hearth.

And why shouldn't it sleep
indoors, after all,
why not?

The days were beautiful
back then, pulled
by two horses across the sky.

NOTES

"Retrato de viuda con caballero andante" draws on a series of Spanish medieval ballads about the *caballero andante*, "knight errant," returning from the Crusades. Typical of oral tradition in general, and medieval ballads in particular, there are many, often conflicting, versions of this story, in which the husband returns from war in disguise and attempts to seduce his wife in order to test her fidelity. While there are many ballad collections, my reading came largely from Antonio G. Solalinde's *Cien romances escogidos*, published by Espasa-Calpe in 1940.

The following lines in "Retrato de viuda" come directly from the version of the ballad I followed in Solalinde's book:

> *Calla, calla, Catalina*
> *Calla, calla de una vez,*
> *Que estás hablando con tu marido*
> *Y no lo sabes reconocer*
> *Que estás hablando con tu marido*
> *Y no lo sabes reconocer.*

My nearly literal translation is as follows:

> *Hush, hush, Catalina*
> *Hush now*
> *You're speaking with your husband*
> *And you don't even recognize him*
> *You're speaking with your husband*
> *And you don't even recognize him.*

It's difficult to translate the nuance of a line like "Y no lo sabes reconocer," where one might also render the line as both "you don't know to recognize him" and "you don't know *how* to recognize him."

The title for "Shed Boat Shed" was inspired by conceptual artist Simon Starling's work, *Shedboatshed*, for which he won the Turner Prize in 2005.

"They Said It Would Hurt, and It Does," takes its title from the last line of Carl Phillip's poem "A Little Closer Though, If You Can, for What Got Lost Here."

ACKNOWLEDGMENTS

Many thanks to the editors of the following journals, wherein these poems first appeared, sometimes in different form:

Black Rabbit Quarterly: "A Brief History of War, From Rome to Present Day"
Copper Nickel: "Retrato de viuda con caballero andante," "How We Manage Since Father Died," and "Son in This Story the Oaks Are Tremendous"
FIELD: "What the Wooden Duck Says When I Can't Sleep at Night," "The Blue Hills," "Love Inside the Snow Globe," and "Origin of Speech"
Ilanot Review: "Famine Road"
Lily Poetry Review: "Portrait of Soldier with Mind Ajar"
Plume: "Soldier's Wife in the Aftermath"

I would like to thank JOYA: AiR at Cortijada los Gázquez and Trison Construction for residencies that provided time, space, and beautiful meals while completing the book; and the Somerville Arts Council for financial support.

For the always intelligent reading of my poems and the manuscript, as well as for caring friendship and encouragement, I am deeply grateful to Martha Collins, Steven Cramer, Cate Marvin, Kevin Prufer, and Anne Riesenberg; additional and special thanks to Sharon Bryan, Teresa Cader, and Hermine Meinhard.

Many thanks to Karen and Michael Braziller, and all those at Persea Books, especially Gabe Fried for insightful editorial guidance and support; and to interns Anneka Johnson, Mia Guidolin, Sidonie Habert, and Hayley Graffunder for their valuable input at all stages.

For their lively inquiry and shared passion for poetry, I thank the participants in my weekly workshop at the VNA Senior Living in Somerville.

Finally, to my family and friends, all of whom have endured the writing of these poems as long as I have, I cannot express gratitude enough; and to Mom and Dad, everything.